# Naming Nine

**There are many ways to describe or name a numeral.**

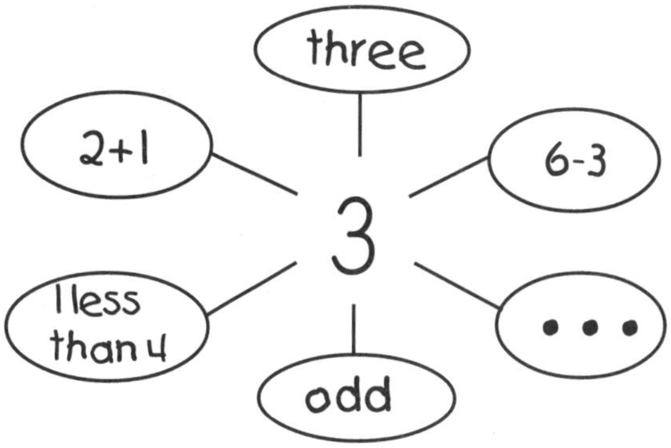

three

2+1

6-3

1 less than 4

odd

• • •

3

Think about the numeral 9.

Show six ways to describe or name it.

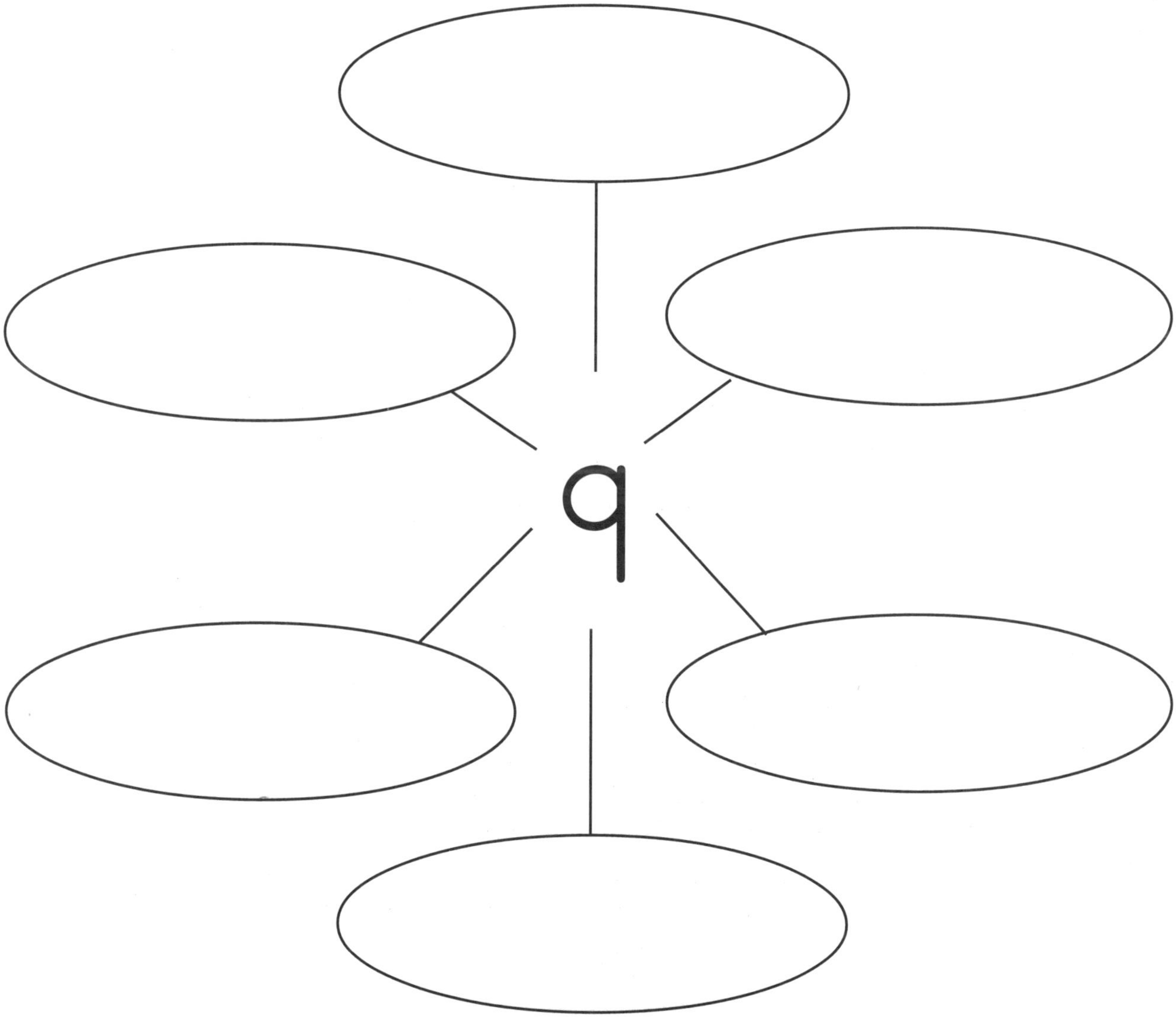

q

# Many Ways to Solve a Problem

Problem:
**I want to give four cookies to everybody at my party.**
**Counting me there will be 9 children at the party.**
**How many cookies do I need to make?**

Solutions:

Use pictures to solve the problem.
Show your work.

Use addition to solve the problem.
Show your work.

Use multiplication to solve the problem.
Show your work.

EMC 4063

# Many Ways to Solve a Problem

Problem:

**I had 96 marbles.**

**I gave 12 marbles to each child.**

**How many children got some marbles?**

Solutions:

Use pictures to solve the problem.

Show your work.

Use subtraction to solve the problem.

Show your work.

Use division to solve the problem.

Show your work.

# Use What You Know

Use what you know about math to match these:

| | |
|---|---|
| half a dozen | 52 |
| pennies in a quarter | three |
| weeks in a year | 6 |
| sides of a pentagon | 25 |
| minutes in an hour | octagon |
| angles on a triangle | 5 |
| shape of a stop sign | sixteen |
| cups in a gallon | 60 |

EMC 4063

# Harvest Time

**We picked vegetables out of the garden today. We filled six baskets.**

**Each basket held five ears of corn, six yellow squash, and four cabbages.**

**How many vegetables were there all together?**

How did you find the answer to this problem?

# How Many Ways Can You Make $1.00?

Use this money table to help you figure out nine of the combinations of coins that can be put together to make exactly $1.00.

| penny | nickel | dime | quarter | half dollar | $ |
|-------|--------|------|---------|-------------|------|
| 100   |        |      |         |             | = $1.00 |
|       | 5      |      | 3       |             | = $1.00 |
|       |        |      |         |             |      |
|       |        |      |         |             |      |
|       |        |      |         |             |      |
|       |        |      |         |             |      |
|       |        |      |         |             |      |
|       |        |      |         |             |      |
|       |        |      |         |             |      |
|       |        |      |         |             |      |
|       |        |      |         |             |      |

EMC 4063

I have 4 coins.  One is a dime, 1/2 are nickels, the last coin is a quarter.
How much money do I have?

I have 12 coins.  Half of the coins are quarters, 1/4 are dimes, and the rest are pennies.  How much money do I have?

I have $2.00.  Half of the money is quarters.
The rest of the money is in these coins:  3/5 are dimes
                                           1/5 are nickels
                                           the rest are pennies

How many do I have?

_____ quarters          _____ nickels

_____ dimes             _____ pennies

# Soccer Practice

Use this information to answer the questions below.

> **19 grown-ups and 74 children came to the practice game.**
> **21 people left after practice was over.**
> **Everyone else stayed for a picnic.**
> **There were 24 people at each picnic table.**
> **All the tables were full.**

1. How many people came to the practice game?

2. After 21 left, how many people stayed for the picnic?

3. How many picnic tables were full?

EMC 4063

# What Is the Question?

We are always asked to answer questions.
Here is your chance to ask the questions.
Write a question to match each of these answers.

| Answer:   **97**   | Answer: **9 o'clock** |
|---|---|
| Question: | Question: |
| Answer:  **a rectangle and two circles** | Answer:  **divide it into fourths** |
| Question: | Question: |
| Answer: **6 boxes of 12** | Answer: **365** |
| Question: | Question: |

# Building a Tree House

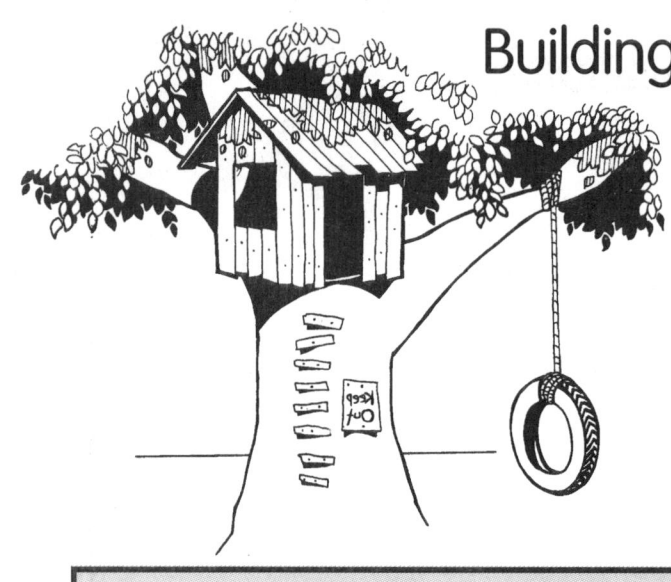

**Carlos, Kisha, and Otto built a tree house in the backyard.**
**Find the answers to these questions about what they did.**

| Problems | Work Space |
|---|---|
| Carlos, Kisha, and Otto needed money to buy materials to build the tree house.<br><br>Carlos did jobs to earn $18.75. Kisha collected cans and bottles to get $9.58. Otto saved his allowance until he had $10.50.<br><br>How much money did they have? | |
| They went to the lumberyard and spent $26.34 for wood, nails, and paint.<br><br>How much money did they have left? | |
| They worked every Saturday for 4 weeks. Each Saturday they worked from 9:30 'till 4:00. They stopped for an hour for lunch each day.<br><br>How much time did they spend building the tree house? | |

EMC 4063

# The Nature Museum

Mom took us to the nature museum. We left home at 9:15. We got to the museum at 9:55. How many minutes did it take to get there?

The museum had a display of insects. We saw:

    25 beetles

    11 dragonflies

    48 butterflies

    32 crickets

How many insects did we see?

In another room we saw stuffed birds. We saw 58 different birds. Half of the birds were from South America. How many birds were from South America?

There were three rooms with large animals. If each room had 12 animals, how many large animals were there in all?

We started looking at animals at 10:00. We had to stop at 1:30. How long had we looked at animals?

The nature museum is open seven days a week. Every day 105 people come to see the animals. How many people come to the museum in one week?

# Think About Pairs

Wouldn't it be strange if these animals wore shoes, socks, and gloves?
How many pair of each thing would they need. Remember a **pair** is **two**.
Zero is a correct answer sometimes.

|  | pairs of socks | pairs of shoes | pairs of gloves |
|---|---|---|---|
| | l |  |  |
| |  |  |  |
| |  |  |  |
| |  |  |  |
| |  |  |  |

12

 # Popcorn!

**I love popcorn! I like it with a lot of butter and a little bit of salt. I like it so much, I used my allowance to buy a big bag of popcorn kernels. I knew my mom would let me use the salt and butter we have at home.**

| | |
|---|---|
| The bag of popcorn kernels cost me 84¢. I gave the clerk at the store $1.00. How much change did I get back? | One cup of popcorn kernels made four cups of popped corn. There were 8 cups of kernels in the bag. How many cups of popped corn did I get? |
| I ate two cups of popcorn every night while I watched television. How many cups did I eat in one week? | Three of my friends came over Saturday to play catch. I make a bowl of popcorn for a snack. If the bowl holds 12 cups of popcorn, how much will we each get to eat? (Don't forget to count me when you answer the questions!) |
| We drank apple juice with our popcorn. We each drank 2 glasses. How much apple juice did we drink? | I started cleaning up the popcorn popper and washing the juice glasses at 4:15. It took me 25 minutes. What time did I finish? |

# My Own Problems

Look at this map.

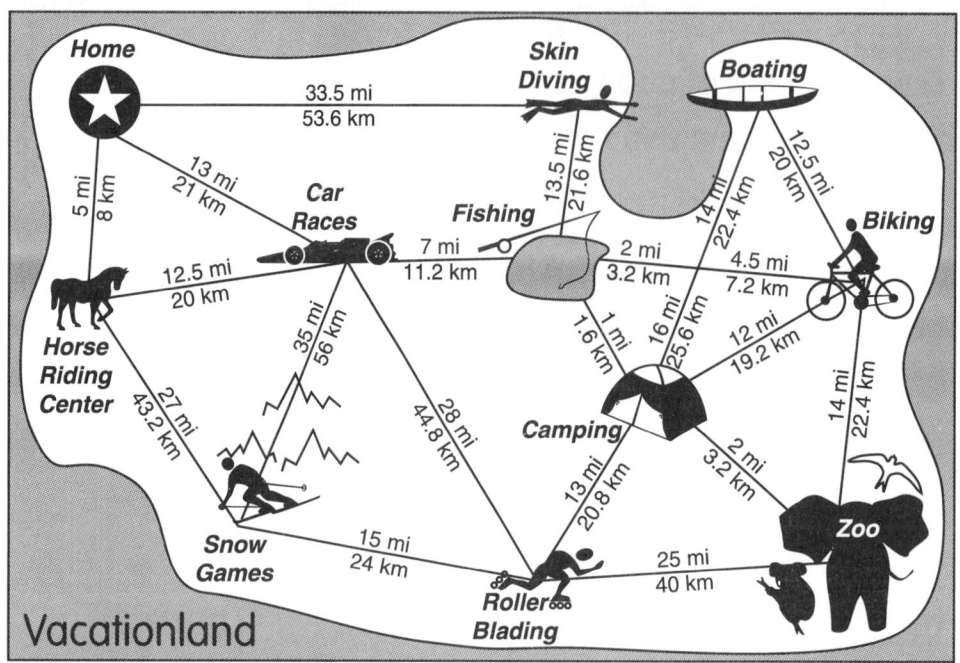

Make up your own problems.

Write the questions and the answers.

| | |
|---|---|
| | |
| | |

EMC 4063

# In Search of Treasure

**Many years ago, pirates buried treasure on a small island in the ocean. Captain Jones found an old map showing where to find the treasure. She and her crew decided to look for the treasure. Find the answers to these problems to help them.**

| Problem | Work Area |
|---|---|
| The crew landed on shore.  They walked 6 miles to a large boulder. They turned left and walked 5 miles to some palm trees.  They rested for the night.  The next day they walked 8 more miles.  How far did they walk? | |
| The crew came to a small lagoon. There was a small hill in the middle of the lagoon.  It took 2 minutes to row to the hill.  It took 6 minutes to climb the hill. It took 43 minutes to dig up the treasure.  How many minutes did all of this take? | |
| When Captain Jones opened the treasure chest, she found 12 bars of gold, 8 long silver chains, and 4 diamond necklaces.  The captain got half of the treasure. How much did she get to keep?<br><br>\_\_\_\_\_ bars of gold<br><br>\_\_\_\_\_ silver chains<br><br>\_\_\_\_\_ diamond necklaces | |

Nuts!

**Welcome to Brown's Nut Shop.**
**We sell all kinds of nuts.**
**Think about these "nutty" questions.**

| | |
|---|---|
| There are 3 coconuts in each box. I have 9 boxes of coconuts. How many coconuts do I have? | I have 108 walnuts to put in these little bags. Each bag holds 9 walnuts. How many bags will I use? |
| If one coconut costs 89 cents, how much will 10 coconuts cost? | Mr. Ruiz bought 8 bags of pecans. There were 36 pecans in each bag. How many pecans did he get? |
| I have 100 jars of peanut butter. I sold one dozen jars each day last week. How many jars do I have left? | Mrs. Yan's women's group made peanut brittle to sell to raise money for charity. They used 1/2 pound of peanuts for each batch. How many pounds of peanuts did they use to make 26 batches? |

# Reading a Calendar

| October | | | | | | |
|---|---|---|---|---|---|---|
| Sun | Mon | Tues | Wed | Thurs | Fri | Sat |
| | | 1 | 2 | 3 | 4 | 5 |
| 6 | 7 | 8 | 9 | 10 | 11 | 12 |
| 13 | 14 | 15 | 16 | 17 | 18 | 19 |
| 20 | 21 | 22 | 23 | 24 | 25 | 26 |
| 27 | 28 | 29 | 30 | 31 | | |

| November | | | | | | |
|---|---|---|---|---|---|---|
| Sun | Mon | Tues | Wed | Thurs | Fri | Sat |
| | | | | | 1 | 2 |
| 3 | 4 | 5 | 6 | 7 | 8 | 9 |
| 10 | 11 | 12 | 13 | 14 | 15 | 16 |
| 17 | 18 | 19 | 20 | 21 | 22 | 23 |
| 24 | 25 | 26 | 27 | 28 | 29 | 30 |

What day of the week is:

October 13 _____

October 22 _____

October 19 _____

October 30 _____

In November what is the date of:

first Saturday _____

last Thursday _____

second Wednesday _____

third Monday _____

How many days in October are school days?

How many days in November are weekend days?

If there are 365 days in one year, how many days will there be in 5 years?

How many months are there in three years?

| Problem | Work Area |
|---|---|
| My number is between 0 and 9.<br>It cannot be divided by 2.<br>It is less than 9 and more than five.<br>What is my number? | |
| My number is less that 20.<br>It is an odd number.<br>It is not a 2-digit number.<br>It is not the number of sides on a triangle.<br>It is not the number of days in a week.,<br>It can be divided by three.<br>What is my number? | |
| My number is between 20 and 40.<br>It is an odd number.<br>Its digits add up to 8.<br>The largest digit minus the smaller<br>digit is 2.<br>What is my number? | |
| Make up your own number puzzle. | |

EMC 4063

# Little League

| Problem | Work Area |
|---|---|
| There are 59 boys and 49 girls in the baseball league this year. If there are 9 teams in the league, how many players will each team have? | |
| Our team had batting practice today. Each player had a chance to swing at 12 balls. If 9 players came to practice, how many balls were pitched? | |
| Last year we had 318 hits during the whole season. This year we had 27 hits in our first game, 12 hits in our second game, and 29 hits in our last game. How many more hits do we need to make this year to have the same total as last year? | |

# Man Takes Flight!

| Problem | Work Area |
|---|---|
| The Wright brothers started trying to build a "flying machine" in 1900.  Their first flight took place in 1903.  How many years did it take them to have a successful flight?<br><br>How many years ago did that flight take place? | |
| The Wright brothers made four flights that day. The shortest flight was 120 feet (42 meters) long. The longest flight was 852 feet (260 meters) long. What was the difference between the two flights? | |
| Wilber Wright was born in 1867. His brother Orville was born in 1871.  How old was each brother in 1903?  How much older was Wilber than Orville?<br><br>In 1903 Wilber was_____<br>In 1903 Orville was_____<br>Wilber was _____ years older than Orville. | |

EMC 4063

# Bikes

| Problem | Work Area |
|---|---|
| Kim's new bike cost twice as much as Bob's.  If Bob's bike cost $189, how much did Kim's cost? | |
| Jill has an old bike.  Her parents gave her $40 to repair it.  New tires will cost $21. She also wants to buy a bell for $5 and a basket for $13. How much money will she have left? | |
| 12 of the children in Jill's class have bikes.  Half of the bikes are red, 1/4 of bikes are blue. The rest the bikes are other colors.<br><br>How many bikes are red?<br>How many bikes are blue? | |

# Spring Vacation

We are out of school for one week for spring break. Help my family solve this problem as we plan our trip to my grandparents' house for a vacation. There are four people in my family. We need to go the cheapest way.

**Should we drive or fly?**

| Problem | Work Area |
|---|---|
| It costs $156 each for us to fly round trip. We could get there in one day. We would also need $12 for a taxi from the airport to my grandparent's house. They will drive us back to the airport. | |
| To drive would cost us $46 for gas and $37 for food each day. It would cost us $40 for a room each day. We could get there in three days and two nights. | |
| Would it be cheaper for us to fly or to drive? How much cheaper? | |

# The Solar System

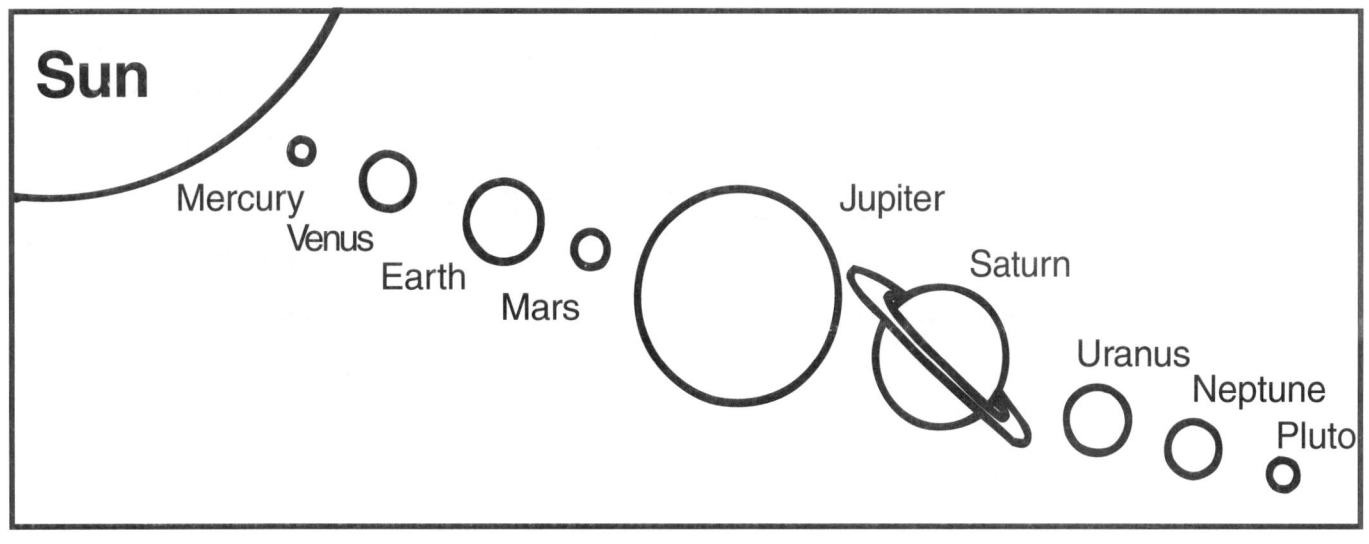

| Problem | Work Area |
|---|---|
| Mercury is 58 million kilometers from the sun.  Earth is 155 million kilometers from the sun. How much farther away from the sun is Earth than Mercury? | |
| The diameter of Earth is 12,756 kilometers. The diameter of Saturn is 120,600 kilometers. The diameter of Uranus is 51,300 kilometers.<br>Is the sum of these three planets more or less than Jupiter's diameter of 142,200 kilometers? How much more or less? | |
| Pluto is 5,900 million kilometers from the sun. How many kilometers would a space ship have to travel to go from Pluto to the sun and back? | |

# Check It Out

Remember: You find the **area** of a shape by multiplication

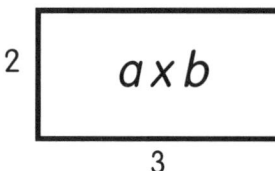

$2 \times 3 = 6$
area is <u>6</u>

You find the **perimeter** of a shape by addition.

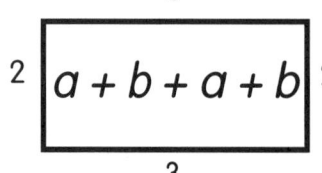

$2 + 3 + 2 + 3$
perimeter is <u>10</u>

You will need a ruler to help you find areas and perimeters.

| | |
|---|---|
| 1. Get a cereal box.<br><br>2. Find the area of the front of the box.<br><br>3. Find the perimeter of the front of the box. | Draw the box here. |
| 1. Get a another box.<br><br>2. Find the area of the front of the box.<br><br>3. Find the perimeter of the front of the box. | Draw the box here. |
| Which box has the larger area? _____<br><br>Which box has the greater perimeter? _____ | |

EMC 4063

# Estimation

**Step 1:**

a. Get a cup of dried beans.

b. Look carefully at the cup.

c. Estimate how many beans are in the cup.

   My estimation is _____ beans are in the cup.

**Step 2:**

a. Put the beans into piles of ten.

b. Count the number of beans you have.

   I have _____ beans.

c. What is the difference between your estimation and the real number of beans?

Get another cup of beans and make a new estimation.
Count the beans to see if your estimation is closer this time.

# A Flower Float

My class at school is making a float for the big spring parade. Our float is going to be a flower garden. We have divided our class into six groups. Each group will do one part of the float. Solve these problems to help us decide what each group needs.

| | |
|---|---|
| Groups One and Two painted the float bed green. Group One painted 2 hours a day for three days. Group Two painted 4 hours on Saturday. How many hours did the two groups paint? | Group Three needs 19 yellow tulips, 16 pink tulips and 22 red tulips. How many tulips do they need? |
| Group Four needs 72 petunias. They bought containers of petunias. Each container holds 6 plants. How many containers did they buy? | Group Five needs 37 daffodils and 29 irises. How many more daffodils than irises did they buy? |
| Group Six needs snapdragons. They bought 6 each of 8 colors. How many snapdragons did they buy? | The parade began at 9:30. It ended at 11:00. How long was the parade? |

EMC 4063

 Dinosaurs

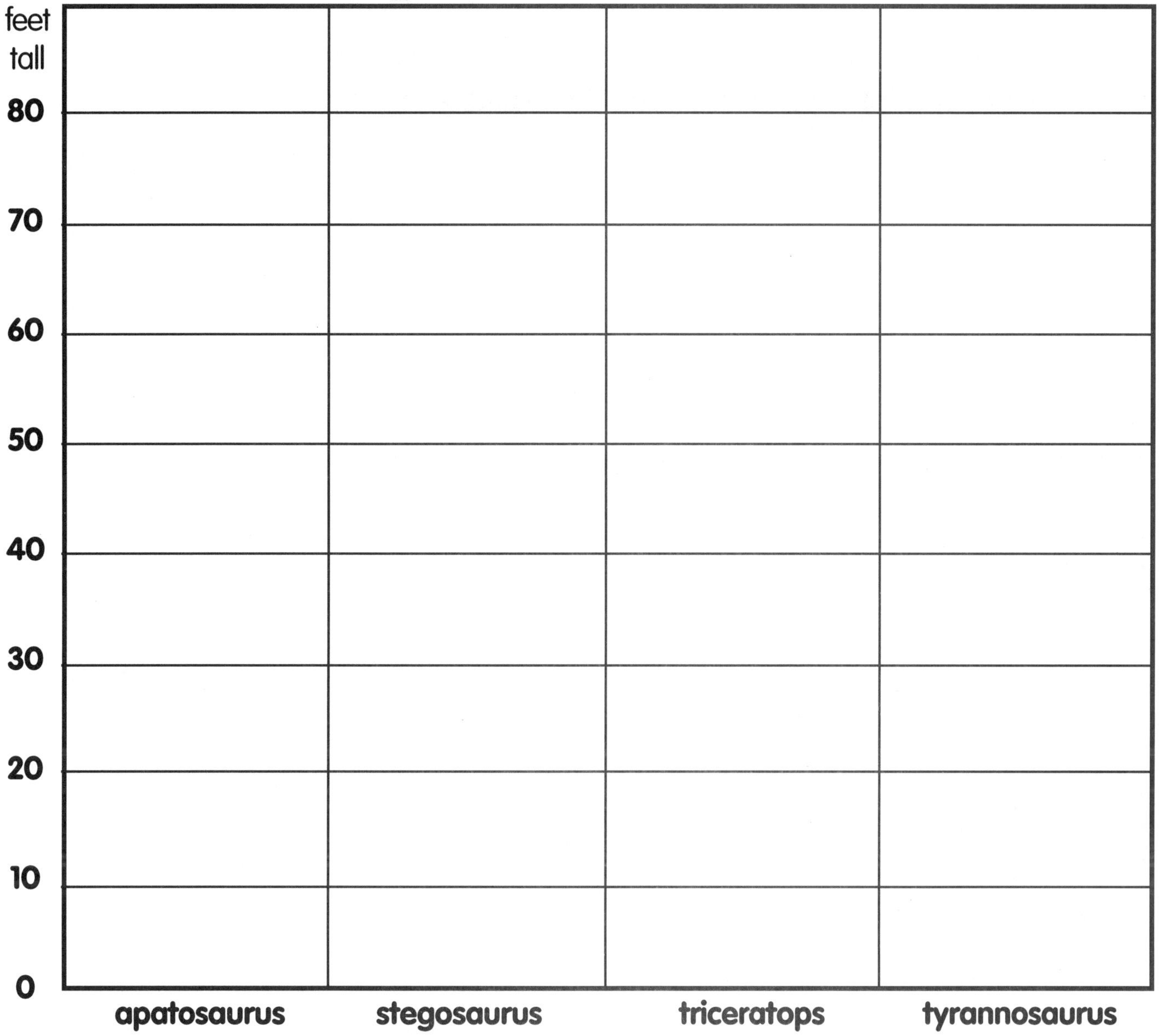

| feet tall | | | | |
|---|---|---|---|---|
| **80** | | | | |
| **70** | | | | |
| **60** | | | | |
| **50** | | | | |
| **40** | | | | |
| **30** | | | | |
| **20** | | | | |
| **10** | | | | |
| **0** | apatosaurus | stegosaurus | triceratops | tyrannosaurus |

Fill in the graph using this information

| 70 feet apatosaurus | 25 feet triceratops |
|---|---|
| 25 feet stegosaurus | 50 feet tyrannosaurus |

Which 3 dinosaurs would equal 100 feet if put together?

_____ _____ _____

# Pie Factory

I work in a pie factory. We make pies for stores and restaurants. Some of the pies are sold whole. Some of the pies are sold already cut into pieces. Think about fractions and think about pies as you do these problems.

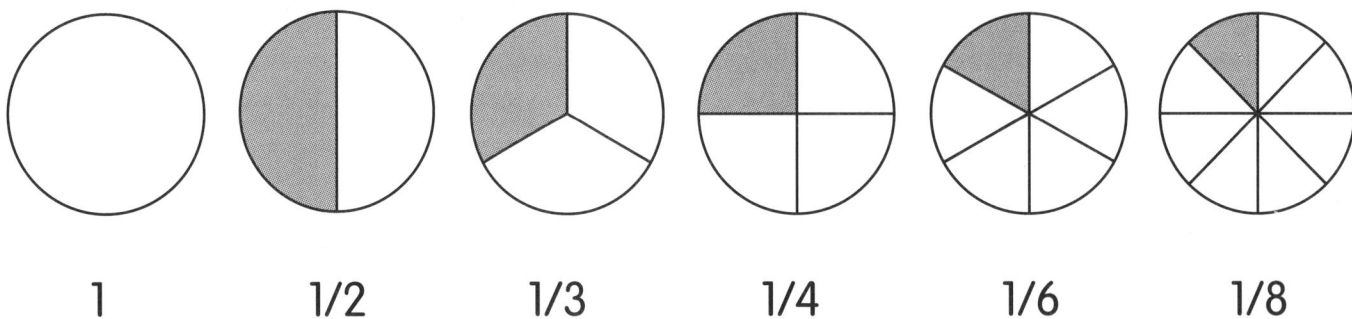

| 1 | 1/2 | 1/3 | 1/4 | 1/6 | 1/8 |

| Problems | Work Space |
|---|---|
| We baked 25 each of lemon, apple, and cherry pies each hour on Monday. If we worked 8 hours, how many pies did we bake? | |
| 9 of the apple pies were cut into fourths. How many pieces of apple pie were there? | |
| 6 of the lemon pies were cut into thirds. How many pieces of lemon pie were there? | |
| 4 of the cherry pies were cut into sixths. How many pieces of cherry pie were there? | |

EMC 4063

# Use What You Know

Use what you know about math to answer these questions:

the number of
thirds in 3 pies ............................................................ 12

half of 5 X 8 ................................................................. 30

the sides of a square
times the sides of a
triangle ....................................................................... 9

twice fifteen ................................................................. 20

months in a year
divided by the number
of items in a pair ......................................................... 35

1/4 of a dozen eggs .................................................... 6

five times the number
of days in a week ........................................................ 3

# How Old Are You?

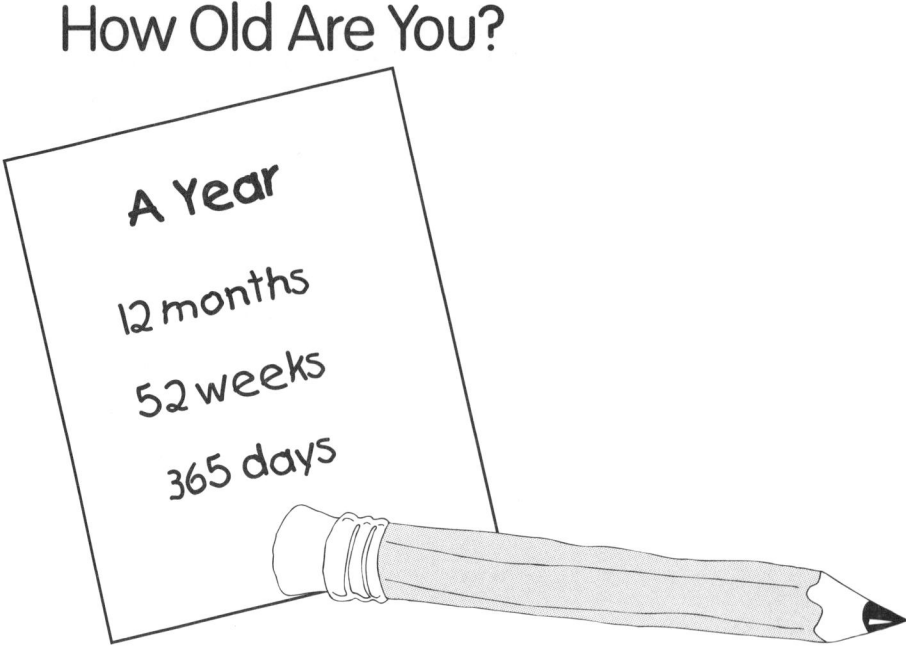

**A Year**

12 months

52 weeks

365 days

Use the information on the chart to figure out how old you are.

I am _____ years old.

I am _____ months old.

I am _____ weeks old.

If you want a really big challenge, try this problem.

I am _____ days old.

EMC 4063

# Answer Key

Please take time to go over the work your child has completed. Ask your child to explain what he/she has done. Praise both success and effort. If mistakes have been made, explain what the answer should have been and how to find it. Let your child know that mistakes are a part of learning. The time you spend with your child helps let him/her know you feel learning is important.

page 1

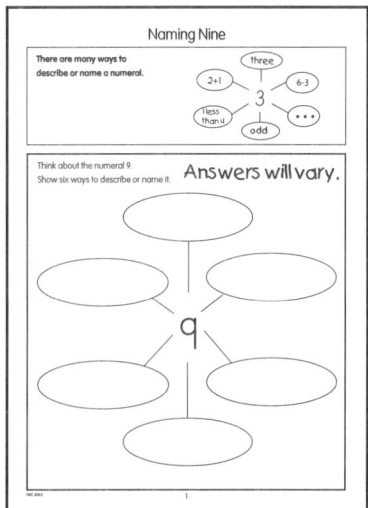

page 2

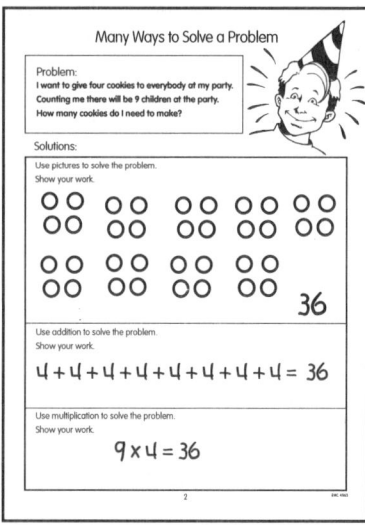

page 3

page 4

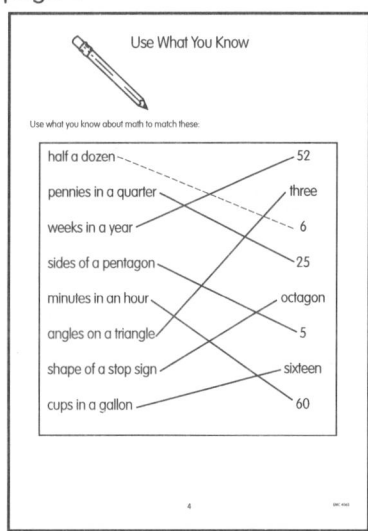

page 5

page 6

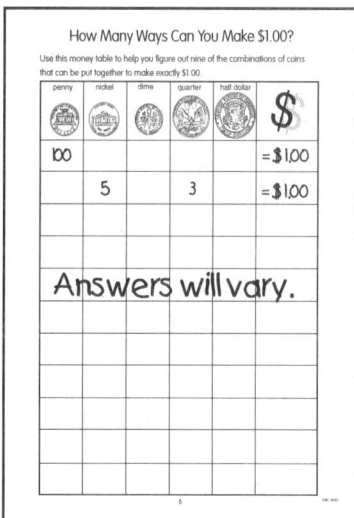

page 7

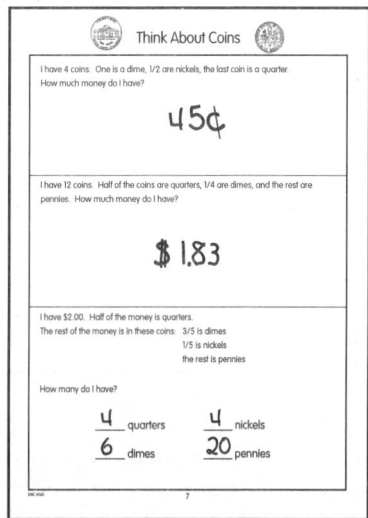

page 8

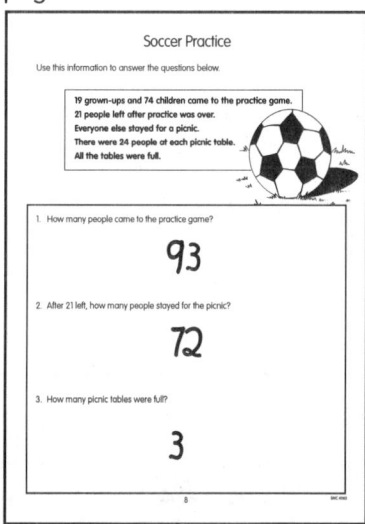

page 9

## page 10

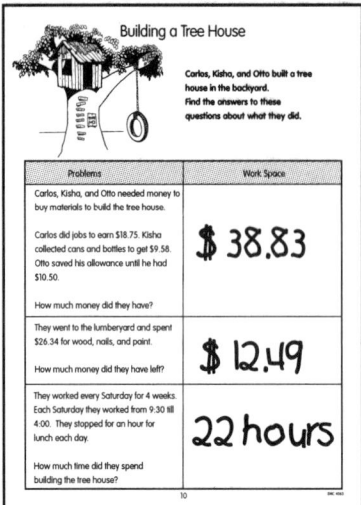

**Building a Tree House**

Carlos, Kisha, and Otto built a tree house in the backyard. Find the answers to these questions about what they did.

| Problems | Work Space |
|---|---|
| Carlos, Kisha, and Otto needed money to buy materials to build the tree house. Carlos did jobs to earn $18.75. Kisha collected cans and bottles to get $9.58. Otto saved his allowance until he had $10.50. How much money did they have? | **$ 38.83** |
| They went to the lumberyard and spent $26.34 for wood, nails, and paint. How much money did they have left? | **$ 12.49** |
| They worked every Saturday for 4 weeks. Each Saturday they worked from 9:30 till 4:00. They stopped for an hour for lunch each day. How much time did they spend building the tree house? | **22 hours** |

## page 11

The Nature Museum

Mom took us to the nature museum. We left home at 9:15. We got to the museum at 9:55. How many minutes did it take to get there?

**40 minutes**

The museum had a display of insects. We saw:
25 beetles
11 dragonflies
48 butterflies
32 crickets
How many insects did we see?

**116**

In another room we saw stuffed birds. We saw 58 different birds. Half of the birds were from South America. How many birds were from South America?

**29**

There were three rooms with large animals. If each room had 12 animals, how many large animals were in all?

**36**

We started looking at animals at 10:00. We had to stop at 1:30. How long had we looked at animals?

**3 1/2 hours**

The nature museum is open seven days a week. Every day 105 people come to see the animals. How many people come to the museum in one week?

**735**

## page 12

Think About Pairs

Wouldn't it be strange if these animals wore shoes, socks, and gloves? How many pair of each thing would they need? Remember a **pair** is **two**. Zero is a correct answer sometimes.

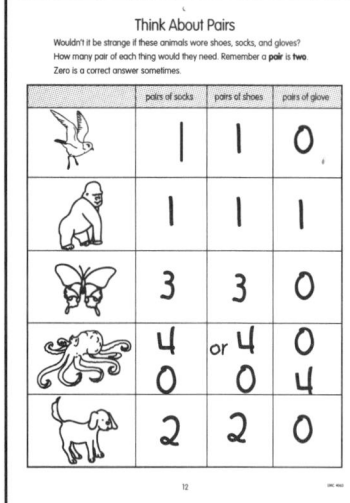

| | pairs of socks | pairs of shoes | pairs of glove |
|---|---|---|---|
| (bird) | 1 | 1 | 0 |
| (gorilla) | 1 | 1 | 1 |
| (butterfly) | 3 | 3 | 0 |
| (octopus) | 4 or 0 | 4 or 0 | 0 or 4 |
| (dog) | 2 | 2 | 0 |

## page 13

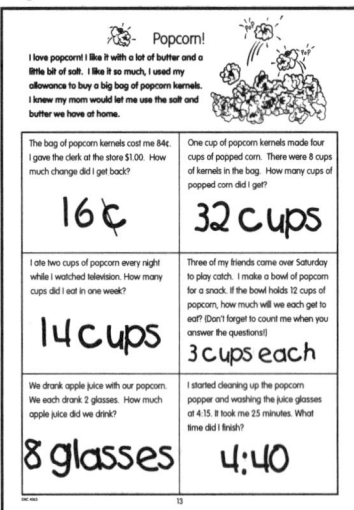

Popcorn!

I love popcorn! I like it with a lot of butter and a little bit of salt. I like it so much, I used my allowance to buy a big bag of popcorn kernels. I knew my mom would let me use the salt and butter we have at home.

| | |
|---|---|
| The bag of popcorn kernels cost me 84¢. I gave the clerk at the store $1.00. How much change did I get back? **16 ¢** | One cup of popcorn kernels made four cups of popped corn. There were 8 cups of kernels in the bag. How many cups of popped corn did I get? **32 cups** |
| I ate two cups of popcorn every night while I watched television. How many cups did I eat in one week? **14 cups** | Three of my friends came over Saturday to play catch. I make a bowl of popcorn for a snack. If the bowl holds 12 cups of popcorn, how much will we each get to eat? (Don't forget to count me when you answer the question!) **3 cups each** |
| We drank apple juice with our popcorn. We each drank 2 glasses. How much apple juice did we drink? **8 glasses** | I started cleaning up the popcorn popper and washing the juice glasses at 4:15. It took me 25 minutes. What time did I finish? **4:40** |

## page 14

My Own Problems

Look at this map.

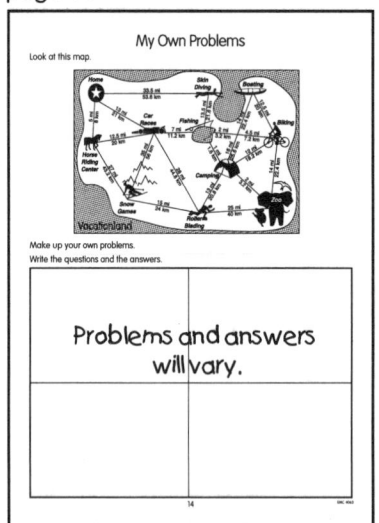

Make up your own problems. Write the questions and the answers.

| | |
|---|---|
| **Problems and answers will vary.** | |

## page 15

In Search of Treasure

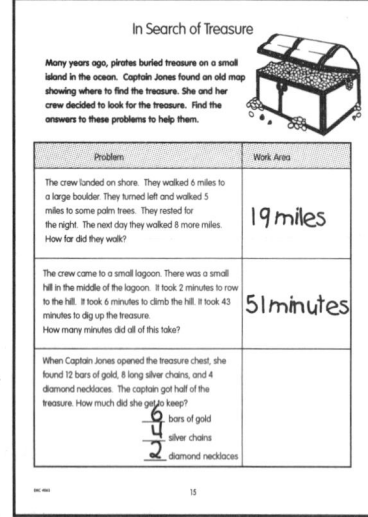

Many years ago, pirates buried treasure on a small island in the ocean. Captain Jones found an old map showing where to find the treasure. She and her crew decided to look for the treasure. Find the answers to these problems to help them.

| Problem | Work Area |
|---|---|
| The crew landed on shore. They walked 6 miles to a large boulder. They turned left and walked 5 miles to some palm trees. They rested for the night. The next day they walked 8 more miles. How far did they walk? | **19 miles** |
| The crew came to a small lagoon. There was a small hill in the middle of the lagoon. It took 2 minutes to row to the hill. It took 6 minutes to climb the hill. It took 43 minutes to dig up the treasure. How many minutes did all of this take? | **51 minutes** |
| When Captain Jones opened the treasure chest, she found 12 bars of gold, 8 long silver chains, and 4 diamond necklaces. The captain got half of the treasure. How much did she get to keep? **6** bars of gold **4** silver chains **2** diamond necklaces | |

## page 16

Parents: If your child has difficulty with any of these problems, encourage him/her to make pictures to help find the answer.

Nuts!

Welcome to Brown's Nut Shop. We sell all kinds of nuts. Think about these "nutty" questions.

| | |
|---|---|
| There are 3 coconuts in each box. I have 9 boxes of coconuts. How many coconuts do I have? **27** | I have 108 walnuts to put in these little bags. Each bag holds 9 walnuts. How many bags will I use? **12 bags** |
| If one coconut costs 89 cents, how much will 10 coconuts cost? **$ 8.90** | Mr. Ruiz bought 8 bags of pecans. There were 36 pecans in each bag. How many pecans did he get? **288 pecans** |
| I have 100 jars of peanut butter. I sold one dozen jars each day last week. How many jars do I have left? **16 jars** | Mrs. Yan's women's group made peanut brittle to sell to raise money for charity. They used 1/2 pound of peanuts for each batch. How many pounds of peanuts did they use to make 26 batches? **13 pounds** |

## page 17

Reading a Calendar

| October | | | | | | | November | | | | | | |
|---|---|---|---|---|---|---|---|---|---|---|---|---|---|
| Sun | Mon | Tues | Wed | Thurs | Fri | Sat | Sun | Mon | Tues | Wed | Thurs | Fri | Sat |

What day of the week is:

October 13 **Sunday**
October 22 **Tuesday**
October 19 **Saturday**
October 30 **Wednesday**

In November what is the date of:

first Saturday **2nd**
last Thursday **28th**
second Wednesday **13th**
third Monday **18th**

How many days in October are school days? **23**

How many days in November are weekend days? **9**

If there are 365 days in one year, how many days will there be in 5 years? **1825**

How many months are there in three years? **36**

## page 18

**8 ? 5** What is My Number? **4 ? 2**

| Problem | Work Area |
|---|---|
| My number is between 0 and 9. It cannot be divided by 2. It is less than 9 and more than five. What is my number? **7** | |
| My number is less that 20. It is an odd number. It is not a 2-digit number. It is not the number of sides on a triangle. It is not the number of days in a week. It can be divided by three. What is my number? **9** | |
| My number is between 20 and 40. It is an odd number. Its digits add up to 8. The largest digit minus the smaller digit is 2. What is my number? **35** | |
| Make up your own number puzzle. **Answers will vary.** | |

EMC 4063